Lightning Source

CHILDREN'S

CLI

LEADERSHIP INSTITUTE

The Children's Leadership Institute,
with help from the Serimus Foundation and Hewlitt Packard,
proudly presents...

Letters from
KATRINA

Stories of Hope & Inspiration

Hoog | Lemaire

Growing Field
Where children go to grow

For information regarding permission contact Growing Field Books at:
311 Belview Ct. Longmont, Colorado 80501
or through info@growingfield.com

**Publisher's Cataloging-in-Publication
(Provided by Quality Books, Inc.)**

Letters from Katrina: stories of hope and inspiration.
p. cm.
LCCN 2007924592
ISBN-13: 978-0-9770391-9-7
ISBN-10: 0-9770391-9-6

1. Hurricane Katrina, 2005 — Correspondence.
2. Hurricane Katrina, 2005 — Pictorial works.
3. Children — Mississippi — Hancock County — Correspondence.
4. Children's writings, American — Mississippi — Hancock County.
5. Hancock County (Miss.) — History — 21st century — Correspondence.
6. Hancock County (Miss.) — History — 21st century — Pictorial works.

F349.H2L48 2007   976.2'14064
                           QBI07-600124

Editor - Mark Hoog
Photography by Kim Lemaire
Cover/Jacket Design by Rob Aukerman
Interior Design by Gwyn Snider

Printed in United States of America

Art is the universal language of children. Through the verbal or written story, children can open a window to their world that only another child can understand. There is no better way for a child to express his or her true feelings to another child. Sharing their experiences with each other through the art of communication is an excellent way for children to teach and learn the lessons in life.

Letters from Katrina is a collection of powerful memories and overwhelming circumstances as seen through the eyes of children that experienced this cataclysmic event. They learned that a neighbor is not just the person next door: we are all neighbors when we help each other in time of need.

Great challenges in life usually bring about great change. Through the pictures and stories of courage, strength, responsibility, perseverance and hope contained in the pages of this book, we learn that change can be for the better.

The spirit of a child is incredibly strong and resilient. In Letters from Katrina, our children tell children around the world that no matter what life brings, we can make it – together!

Marsha Barbour

First Lady, Mississippi

It is with great pride and excitement that I share with you the *Letters From Katrina* story. What began as a small classroom of elementary students working on a project for survivors of Hurricane Katrina has grown into a powerful reminder for the nation that each of us can change the world by sharing with others the promise of the future.

Letters From Katrina is not another picture book profiling the destruction caused by Hurricane Katrina. It is not about looking back in fear or placing blame. Rather it is an opportunity to view the world through the eyes of a child once again to see a world filled with hope, compassion and possibility.

As the author of the Growing Field children's leadership series, I spend much of my time in classrooms across the country speaking with children about the message found in each of my stories...life is without limit! Wanting to share this same message with students along the Gulf after Hurricane Katrina, the decision was made to visit schools in Mississippi and give to them book one from the Growing Field series...*Your Song*.

Before leaving for Mississippi a visit was made to a local elementary school in Ft. Collins, Colorado where students were asked to inscribe a message inside the books to a friend in Mississippi. Asked only to search their hearts for what they would say to a friend who had lost everything in Hurricane Katrina, the children began writing. In doing so, they produced a gift of their own... One that carried meaning for a much larger audience. That day, inside a third grade classroom, *Letters From Katrina* was born.

Delivering the books and speaking to students throughout Southern Mississippi, I was accompanied by California photographer Kim Lemaire. Through the magic of photography Kim captured the smiles, the giggles and the innocence of those most affected by Hurricane Katrina. Through her lens Kim was able to capture the emotion of the children and brought a powerful visual to the *Letters From Katrina* vision.

Excitement for the project grew as additional students, classrooms and schools requested to participate with letters of their own. The project resulted in the donation of over $20,000 of Growing Field books, spread from Colorado to California, generated thousands of letters to and from children in Mississippi and opened the door to a lifetime of friendship opportunities.

In the opening pages of *Letters From Katrina* elementary students from Mississippi share with you their Hurricane Katrina experience. One writes of swimming from a roof top, through muddy storm waters, to a rescue boat. Others share the fear and frustration that comes when a rising storm surge takes with it everything in sight and leaves only uncertainty. The heart of the book contains pen pal letters written between children sharing their dreams, offering one another hope, and providing each other encouragement.

Today, along the Gulf Coast, the winds have subsided and the flood waters receded, leaving behind *Letters From Katrina*. Let each letter serve as a powerful reminder that we must learn to look past "what is" if we are ever to see "what is possible." Let the words of children remind us that none of us are "haves" so long as there are "have-nots." Visit your childhood again and recall the magic that occurs when we ask not about skin color, gender, religion or socio-economic status but instead ask the one question that will truly change the world… "Will you be my friend?"

I want *Letters From Katrina* to inspire our nation and every letter to serve as a reminder of the contribution each of us can make. I also want the children of Bay St. Louis, Mississippi to understand their future, and their educational opportunities, are without limit. To that end, **100% of all *Letters From Katrina* profits are being donated** to the Katrina Endowment which will provide scholarship opportunities for the children in Bay St. Louis, Mississippi. For additional information on the Katrina endowment, or to make your tax deductible donation, please visit www.lettersfromkatrina.com.

Through *Letters From Katrina* the children remind us of the simple contribution each of us can make. The children naturally share the gift of hope, compassion, encouragement, inspiration and friendship… and believe they can change the world. In the immortal words of John Denver; *It is here we must begin to seek the wisdom of the children.*

Whatever inspiration or wisdom you seek in literature… Whatever promise you hope most to find in our youngest generation… Whatever you want most to believe about the future of our nation… I hope you find it here in the *Letters From Katrina*.

Mark Hoog

Editor

It is here we must begin... to seek the wisdom of the children

John Denver/ Singer, Song writer ~ Rhymes and Reasons

This book is dedicated
to the children who survived Hurricane Katrina...

The message offered by children across our great country is dedicated to you.

To Isabelle!
Josie -
Dream BIG!

Letters from KATRINA

Stories of Hope & Inspiration

"August 29, 2005 was the scariest day of my life I hope that we NEVER ever have another hurricane."

Camaryn – age 11

HURRICANE KATRINA HIT THE GULF COAST ON AUGUST 29, 2005

"It was terrifying."

The storm was horrible. My family stayed in our home and it was terrifying. During the storm we did not think we were going to survive. We all thought that if we died, at least we would all die together as a family. We said lots of prayers as the storm raged with terror outside. I couldn't stop crying.

Our house was in great shape and it protected us from the storm. There was a lot of metal flying around and landing in trees. Our mailbox was destroyed.

The winds were horrible and we lost electricity. It was hot and scary but we had plenty of food to eat. We ate ham, bread and other food that the army gave us. The only drinks we had were sprites, coke and bottled water.

We survived Hurricane Katrina but hope to never see anything like it again.

Alexander W. — age 10

5

Darius Wyman

Age 9

Hurricane Katrina was a bad storm. My family almost died. A tree fell right on the top of our house. My whole family was very very scared. The world was sad. Some people were looking at their houses, some people got diseases from bugs after Hurricane Katrina. The world was shocked. I was shocked. My family and I were sad. I felt bad for the people that died. I was mad. I hated Hurricane Katrina.

THE HURRICANE CAUSED SEVERE DESTRUCTION ACROSS THE ENTIRE MISSISSIPPI COAST

Samantha
Hancock County
Age 10

Days before the storm hit, my family evacuated. We went to Alabama. My aunt, my uncle, and my two cousins stayed here in Bay St. Louis. I was scared for them.

It was a few days before we returned to Bay St. Louis. When we returned I saw some pretty horrible things. I saw cars flipped over, there was a boat in the drive thru at Burger King, and my house was full of grey sticky mud. My room was a mess. Everything was tipped over and my television was busted. I was very sad. I could not believe my eyes.

The days after the storm were tough. I remember taking a bath in a toy box with water from the fire hydrant. We had to eat MRE's and drink bottled water. I did not like some of the food, it tasted weird. We had to sleep outside on couches from inside.

The best thing about the storm was that my family was ok. The worst thing about the storm was it destroyed my house, my school, my town. Things will never be the same.

Samantha H. — age 10

"Things will never be the same."

AT LEAST 1,836 PEOPLE LOST THEIR LIVES

Alexis
North Bay
Age 9

North Bay Elementary School

The STORM
Austin A. – Age 9

9:00 on Sunday night, my mom called me. She was worried about me and the storm. She left with my sister. I stayed in Bay St. Louis with my grandma and my uncle. I remember telling her, " I LOVE YOU" and that I would be praying for us all. She was crying and very upset.

It was 5:00 on Monday morning when we lost electricity. I was asleep and didn't know we lost power. I woke up because I heard the wind. We were scared and worried about the storm. At 9:00 on Monday, the house started to flood. When I saw the water coming into the house I was very nervous. We kept the doors closed as tight as we could. Finally, when the water receded outside we began to sweep the house out and we saw large tree that had fallen in the back yard. I was so nervous I threw up.

THE STORM IS RESPONSIBLE FOR AN ESTIMATED $81.3 BILLION DOLLARS IN DAMAGE

Charlie
North Bay
Age 10

Nathaniel
Hancock County
Age 9

"Before the storm – Big school, Big house, Plenty of friends.
After the storm – Smaller school, Smaller house, Less friends."

Preston H

HURRICANE KATRINA WAS THE COSTLIEST NATURAL DISASTER IN U.S. HISTORY

...THE WINDS CAME UNOBSTRUCTED OFF THE WATER, DRIVING A WALL OF WATER 20-35 FEET HIGH

"The roof had blown off and almost everything was destroyed. I renamed one of my stuffed animals Katrina because it survived the storm."

Alexis — age 9

Natalie
Hancock County
Age 9

The Big Hurricane
by Tyrese

Hurricane Katrina destroyed lives. I left Mississippi on the day of the Hurricane, August 29, 2005. A lot of roads were blocked. We got there before it happened. We stayed there for 3 months. Then came another Hurricane. After that, school was open and a lot of people came. When I got home, I did my homework and then I watched T.V. and North Bay was on T.V. But before it happened I was sad because I knew what will happen. It was just unbelievable.

"Hurricane Katrina destroyed lives."

MORE THAN 57 SHELTERS WERE ESTABLISHED IN COASTAL COMMUNITIES

Alan
(also pictured on the cover)
Mississippi
Age 9

"I felt sad and afraid... many people died."

HURRICANE KATRINA HAD SUSTAINED WINDS OF OVER 175 MPH

We can change lives when we share...

Hope

The living conditions brought on by Hurricane Katrina would tempt anyone to lose hope. Many of the children in Hancock County swam to safety during the storm and then lived on the dirt (or in 8 x 8 storage sheds) with their families waiting for temporary housing.

Today, two years later, most still live (and attend school) in a FEMA trailer. School days begin early as children are bussed inland twenty-five minutes. The state provides breakfast and lunch. Many students go without supper.

The following letters from students in Colorado and California brought more than ear to ear smiles. They also brought messages reminding the students in Mississippi to never give up on themselves or in the future.

The same letters remind us all that hope for the future is the most powerful gift we can give one another.

Gaving Hope

Katriha she was big and strong
Why did it last so long
came at you with all her force

Hope

Hope is what we had

Once we saw it on the news

I gave my hope to you

when I wrote this Poem
All I could think about
was helping you not to be
blue.

by Khristy

Megan
Hancock County
Age 8

Your hopes and dreams are not lost. Your song is still with you. I am praying for you.

Your friend in Fort Collins,

Jasmine

IF YOU FOLLOW YOUR DREAMS, YOUR HOPES AND WISHES WILL COME TRUE. - SCOTT G. AGE 10

Samuel
Hancock County
Age 10

Dear Mississippi friend,

I can't imagine how hard it is for you. I've heard about how hard it is and I feel really bad. Hopefully, your life will get better and your dreams will come true in the future. I hope you don't think that your alone, because you can write to me all of the time. Even though you've lost every thing; that doesn't mean that you have to stop beleiving. You're really strong for going through this, but you're even stronger in your heart. You can do so much in the future so don't give up. I hope that your life gets better. Your in my prayers.

Your Colorado friend,

Sara

You'll fufill your dreams

I WISH YOU OVER 100 SMILES, LUCK, AND LOVE. I'M ALWAYS HERE. - GRACE H. AGE 11

Paul
Mississippi
Age 10

Dear Mississippi Friend,

I am sorry what happened to you. Just soar with the wind. Keep your hopes high. I believe in you. Please write to me. I will try to write back.

Sincerely,

Lindsay
Traut Core Knowledge School

IF THERE IS ANYTHING I CAN DO FOR YOU...I AM THERE FOR YOU!   - MADELEINE G. 5TH GRADE

Julissa
Mississippi
Age 10

September 8, 2006

Dear Mississippi friend,

I hope you are okay. I'm very sorry that Hurricane Katrina ruined your town. There is always hope in life. I hope this book makes your dreams come true.

La!

Your Friend,
Rebecca

Ayshia
Mississippi
Age 10

Dear Mississippi friend,
I hope you don't think that you're alone, because you can write to me whenever. You can do so much, so don't give up hope! I am praying for you. And remember, the sun will always shine on you.

From,
Kylie age 9
CALIFORNIA

Madelynn
Hancock County
Age 11

O'Dea Elementary
312 Princeton Rd
Ft Collins CO 80525

When you read this story, I hope you have a smile on your face.

Love,

Elianna

Dear Mississippi Student,

My Name is Emily _____ I am from Fort Collins Colorado. I am an 8 year old girl, and I am here to suport you. I want to tell you still have courage in your heart and that will never leave you, because it is that is farthest down in you. I wish you luck though we may live far away. I may not be able to wrap up a present with a bow but I can still send you luck my heart.

Sincerly, Emily

Dear Mississippi Friend,

I hope you are doing ok.
I will pray for you every day.
I am sending you my love and I hope
you will be safe forever.
I hope all your dreams come true.

Love,
Mike

"I hope all your dreams come true."

I AM ALWAYS INTERESTED IN WHAT YOU HAVE TO SAY ABOUT YOUR LIFE. - NATASHA F. 5TH GRADE

Samantha
Hancock County
Age 9

Tyler
Mississippi
Age 10

"I hope you are well... You will be in my prayers."

Dear Mississippi Friend,

I hope you are well. I can't imagine what you are going through. It must be pretty bad down there, and I feel really bad. I have heard that it is really bad. Alway belive and strive for your dreams. You will be in my prayers. Best wishes!! :)

Your Friend,

Vivienne

YOU ARE UNIQUE IN YOUR OWN WAY AND YOU'LL SUCCEED AT MANY THINGS, I GUARANTEE IT. - SARA M. AGE 10

Anthony
Hancock County
Age 10

Austin
North Bay
Age 10

Dear Mississippi Friend,

I hope you are doing better than during Katrina. I know times have been hard for you, but you should still follow your hopes, dreams, and goals. Katrina may have taken things from you, and I'll give this book and my compassion. Katrina is a turn in life, but you've got to keep trying for your dreams. I hope life gets better and you can get a new home. We in Fort Collins haven't forgot about you. Remember we care about you from California to Maine, so don't give up hope my friend. We have faith in you th you will get better. I hope your paycheck can buy a car or a house.

Faith

"Get better!"

Your Friend,
Joshua

"Follow your hopes, dreams, and goals!"

"We believe in you!"

P.S. Write Back

"All I can give is compassion!"

"We haven't forgot!"

Care

"I hope you are doing well!"

Hope

"Remember... we care about you!"

ALTHOUGH WE ARE FAR APART I'M ALWAYS THERE FOR YOU. - AUDREY O. 3RD GRADE

We can change communities when we offer...

Encouragement

Many of the children in Hancock County still suffer from Post Traumatic Stress Disorder. During the storm one little girl was orphaned and many others were separated from their parents- unsure if they would see them again.

For many children the problems are just beginning as they come to realize life will never again be the same.

The books delivered to the students in Mississippi, in many cases, represented the first new book they had ever received. The pen pal letter found inside brought stickers, pictures and laughter.

Most importantly they brought words of encouragement and remind us all that sometimes belief in another, until they can again believe in themselves, is the most powerful gift we can ever give.

Dear Friend

We all believe in you. You can make your place a better place. Just don't give up.

Your Friends,
Matthew

"We all believe in you."

I THINK ABOUT YOU, I PRAY FOR YOU AND CARE ABOUT YOU. - SAMUEL T. 5TH GRADE

Paul
Hancock County
Age 9

Shaylynn
Hancock County
Age 10

Believe in yourself. Never give up when things are hard, just remember you are a TALENTED person so whatever is inside of YOU let it come out.

So don't worry you'll be blooming soon enough. Now fing your song, to SOAR!

You ☀ are

a

Blooming flower

♡ Maria

"You are a talented person."

"Always a rainbow after a storm."

Dear Mississippi Friend,

I know I may never experience something this terrible but, somehow I can tell everything will work out!!! Just remember there is always a rainbow after a storm!!! What I mean is something so bad ~~████~~ like a hurricane can be made into something good like new friends. Just be strong and make the best out of it! Remember our entire country is thinking of you!!! You may not know me and I don't really know you quite yet but I can tell we are going to be great friends!!!

Your friend/pen pal,

Annalee

California

P.S. I can't wait to get to know you!!!!!!!

YOU'VE GOT TO TEAR DOWN THE WALLS OF CONVENTION WITH A WRECKING BALL OF CREATIVITY. - JOHN C. 5TH GRADE

"Everyone... is there for you."

To: My friend in the Hurricane Katrina, I want to let you in on a little secret. There will be a time in your life where some one or something bad happens to you. But just remember Shepardson and every one else is there for you.

Sincerely,
your
friend,
Sierra

I FEEL LIKE HUGGING YOU. - HALEY O. AGE 11

Macey
Mississippi
Age 9

Dear friend,

I would like to give you a letter to show my friendship. To give a letter of gratitude. To show you that you can change the world. That you have a very special talent. Express your talent, Show that you can do anything. You can make a difference. So show your song.

You friend,
Christopher

"Everyone... is there for you."

To: My friend in the Hurricane Katrina, I want to let you in on a little Secret. There will be a Time in your life where Some one or Something bad happens to you. But Just remember Shepardson and every one else is there for you.

Sincerely,
your
friend,
Sierra

I FEEL LIKE HUGGING YOU. - HALEY O. AGE 11

Dear Mississippi Friend,

You are still remembered. Keep dreaming big and believing in yourself. I know you will get through these hard times. Thinking about you and your family warms my heart.

⭐Your fan friend, ♡
♡Mckinzie

"Keep dreaming big."

EVEN THOUGH YOU DON'T KNOW ME I HOPE WE CAN BE FRIENDS. I CARE ABOUT YOU. - KYLE W. 5TH GRADE

Elijah
HancockCounty
Age 10

Anthony
Mississippi
Age 10

Good Luck in the future.
Things are always brighter the next day.
keep smiling an things will get better.
I wish you happy and positive thoughts.
zach

"Things are always
brighter the next day."

Dear Mississippi Friend,

Right now we were watching a video of the Katrina incident, I was wondering how you are feeling right now? Are you alright? I feel really sad for you, because we had never had a super bad hurricane come to Monterey before. My name is Nathan Ray B., what's your name?

Sincerely your pen pal,
Nathan

"Everything will work out."

I PRAY FOR YOU, ASKING GOD TO HELP YOU. - TRENTON W. AGE 10

Jack
Hancock County
Age 8

2\11\07

Dear Mississippi friend,

I hope you feel better after the hurricane Katrina. I hope you can rebuild quickly.

your friend
Chris

Katelin
North Bay
Age 10

Dear Mississippi friend,

You inspire me so much! Your my hero. Your stronger than Superman not only in your body but in your heart. Even though we are miles apart your one of the best and amazing friends and peron thats alive. Even though you don't have a lot you'll always have me and you can always trust me. Never stop dreaming. IF you want to know my dream it's for you to be ok..!

You →

Hope you are and will be O.K.,
Christopher

We can change the world when we ask for...

Alora
Hancock County
Age 10

Friendship

Most of the FEMA trailers these children still call home are not waterproof. When it rains local Wal-Mart stores still open their doors to provide a dry environment for the victims of Hurricane Katrina.

Less than 20% of the children in Mississippi can afford to attend college. For these students comfort and shelter come not from living conditions or the promise of the future... but from friendships made.

Out of fear many of the students have not been to the beach since Hurricane Katrina. In this section, photographed on the beach during a special cleanup day, the children of Mississippi once again discover the serenity offered by the same water that brought destruction only two years ago.

While the storm waters changed the lives of these children forever... it also serves as a powerful reminder of the most important bond that unites the human race... Friendship.

When I heard about
the tragic disaster I felt bad, so I wanted to send you a message.
"I hope you and your city rebuild fast. You just have to stick in there
but you don't have to do it alone. I'm there for you." Even through we
live very far apart I still care about you. I hope you care about
me and maybe someday become my friend.

Sincerely your new friend,

Morgan

Peace Dove

"We can be friends."

YOU MIGHT HAVE LOST THINGS, BUT YOU HAVE NOT LOST HOPE FROM ME AND EVERYONE IN THE U.S.A. - WALTER B. 5TH GRADE

Kimberly and Jeremy
Hancock County
Age 11

Dear Katie,

My name is Miranda, but you can call me Mimi. I'M 8 about to turn 9 in 1 week. My favorite colors are pink, purple, gold, and silver.

The storm took my home. The funny part is that the storm took the homes but not the parks. The water was over my roof. I cried. I lost

Your pinpal,
my moms friend.
Miranda

Dear Miranda,
I live in Carmel Valley with my dad. My parents are divorced. I live in Monterey with my mom. My favorite color is purple. The beach is great, but the water is _freezing!_ I _love_ to read, swim, and my favorite meal is orange chicken. My favorites list!

singer— Kelly Clarkson
subject in school— literature
board game— Apples to Apples
book— Harry Potter Series

I got a whole bunch of other favorites too! But I don't want to list them all. There is so many! My friends tell me I'm funny, I don't think so! Keep Smilin'!
from
Katie

"What is your name?"

Danielle and Skyler
Hancock County
Age 9

Dear Gavin,

Thank you for the book mark and letter. I also liked the other staff too, You are a good artist! I like Star Wars too, I like soccer and pizza. I'm eleven, I go to All counts. I'm glad you and your house are okay. I can't wait to get to know more about you.

Sinceriley, Matt

Dear Matthew

My name is Gavin. I like base ball, fishing, and hunting. My favorite baseball team is the Alant Braves. My favorite fish is trout and my favorite deer to hunt is white tailed deer. My favorite food is hamburgers. I also like video games and movies. My favorite game is Outdoor Adventures which is a deer hunting and a fishing game. My favorite movie is Star-Wars. I also like drawing. Some people says that I am a good artist. I live in Bay St. Louis Mississippi.

During the storm my house was flooded. We had fish everywhere where, but they were all feashwater fish. There was a big catfish in our house. The fish out side was bass and brim. Hurricane Katrina was a bad storm. It took a year to get back in our house and we are still working on it.

What sport do you like? Do you play any sports? What do you like to do.? What do you like to eat.? What school do you go to and do you like it? I go to Second Street Elemetary and I like it. I am 11. How old are you?

Sincerely,
Gavin

"How old are you?"

I WISH I WAS THERE TO COMFORT YOU. - ELIZABETH T. AGE 10

Cousins Tyrese
and Delfred
North Bay
Age 11

Dear Mississippi Friend,

I hope you are doing well with the [...]
When the hurricane hit, my school and I h[...]
praying for you in chapel. Don't give [...]
you hope, I am encouraging you to [...]
strong and don't give up.

Your new
Pinpal,
Maris

Dear Maris,

When Hurricana Katrina hit down here in Mississippi it was terrible. The only Place I could stay with was my mom and dad. It was scary because the lighting, rain and also that bad wind. The wind sounded like ghost and gools houling.

After the storm was over Mississippi trash, houses, and other things were all over everywhere. People from different compaines tried to clean up all over different places. I am so glad we can still live in Mississippi.

I can remember all sorts of things that hapend here. There was animals walking around looking for food and water. People were trying to build back homes to.

Mississippi has changed because it is cleaner and the stores are being built back. Most people are trying to help clean up.to.

I would love to be your pen pal because I would like to know about each others lives.

Love Hannah,

"Where do you live?"

IF I COULD GO SOMEWHERE I WOULD COME TO VISIT YOU. I THINK ABOUT YOU ALL THE TIME. - KYLIE H. 5TH GRADE

Left to right – Lauren, La Shae, Iris
Mississippi, Age 10

Dear Mackenzie,

My name is Alexis Marie   . I am 8 years old. My favorite animals are dogs and cats. My favorite colors are blue and purple. My favorite sport is basketball. My favorite football team is The Saints.

The Hurricane was horrible. It destroyed homes. A lot of people were flooded and hurt. I lost my house.

What are your favorite animals, colors and sports? What is your favorite football team? What is your middle name?

Your pen pal,
Alexis

Dear Mississippi Friend,

Hurricane Katrina made such a disaster and I want to try to help! I hope you get to go to college! How old are you? What have you lost? When is your birthday? What is your favorite thing? Just wanted to tell you that your in our thoughts and prayers.

Your friend,

Mackenzie D.

P.S. Please write back

"You are in my thoughts."

KEEP TRYING AND EVERYTHING WILL BE OKAY! THE WISH YOUR HEART MAKES WILL COME TRUE. - BRICHON J.

I do want to say in touch with my pen pal because it is nice for people to have new friends.

Loretta

You may have lost everything you've got, but our friendship will never be lost.

Rey

"Our friendship will never be lost."

BE STRONG AND FOLLOW YOUR DREAMS AND DEEPEST DESIRES. EVERYONE BLOSSOMS IN THEIR OWN WAY. - CORTNEE R. AGE 11

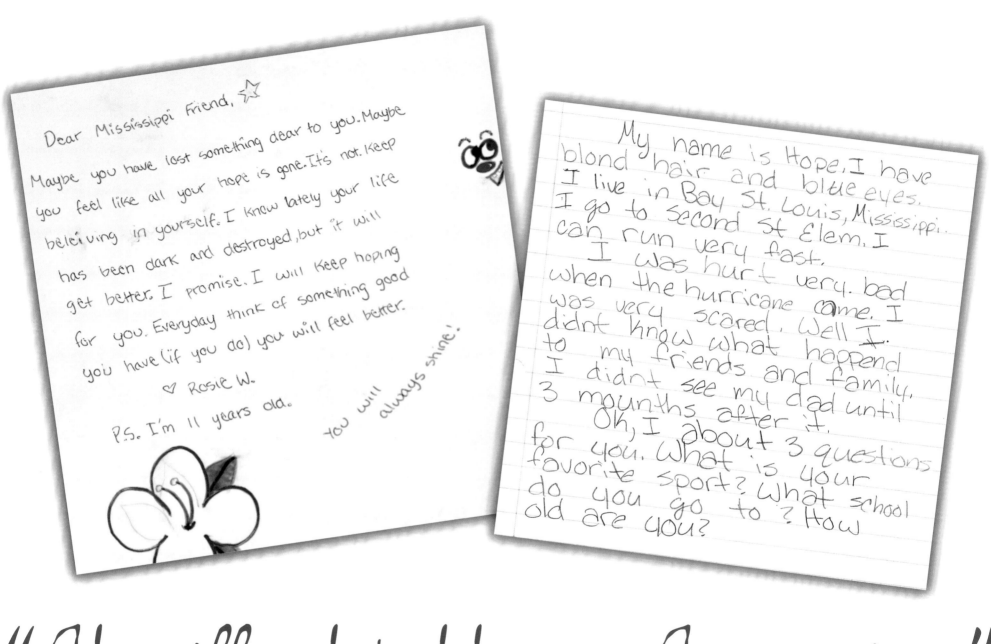

Dear Mississippi Friend, ☆

Maybe you have lost something dear to you. Maybe you feel like all your hope is gone. It's not. Keep beleiving in yourself. I know lately your life has been dark and destroyed, but it will get better. I promise. I will Keep hoping for you. Everyday think of something good you have (if you do) you will feel better.

♡ Rosie W.

P.S. I'm 11 years old.

You will always shine!

My name is Hope. I have blond hair and blue eyes. I live in Bay St. Louis, Mississippi. I go to Second St Elem. I can run very fast.

I was hurt very bad when the hurricane came. I was very scared. Well I didnt know what happend to my friends and family. I didnt see my dad until 3 mounths after it.

Oh, I about 3 questions for you. What is your favorite sport? What school do you go to? How old are you?

"It will get better... I promise."

REMEMBER TO NEVER LOSE HOPE AND ALWAYS BELIEVE IN YOURSELF -BRANDON L. AGE 12

Miranda and Ashanti
Mississippi
Age 11

Dear Mississippi Friend,

I am very sad for you.

All my hopes are for you guys.

I hope your feeling good.

I am sorry you had a hurricane **don't give up on your dreams.**

your friend,

Jack Z

P.S.

What do you wish I said.

Dear Jack Z,

My name is Zoe.
I am 8 years old. My favorite animals are ferrets.

I lost every thing in Hurricane Katrina Toys, pictures, and books. At first I lost hope then I grew it back. My house is almost done but my heart is still broken because every thing of every thing I lost. I still have my memories but not the stuff I have memories about.

Enough about me! Whats your last name! favorite color, and favorite Animal?

"Don't give up."

IF TIMES GET HARD AND NEED A FRIEND I'LL ALWAYS WRITE BACK. BELIEVE IN YOURSELF.   - WILL T. 5TH GRADE

Morgan And Gabrielle
North Bay
Age 10

Dear mississippi Friend,

I'm sorry that the hurricane happened to your town.
I hope you get a new home and toys. I'm in second
grade and I live in Colorado. I would like to Be
your friend. I will pray for you and your family
every day. I hope you like this book!

love,
mitchell

Febuary 13, 2007

Dear Friend,

Thank you for the letters.
I appisliat it. You are best fiend
ever. North Bay Elementry was
Destoyd. Evexthing in Mississippi was
destoyd. the house fell over

EVEN THOUGH WE ARE FAR APART YOU ARE MY FRIEND. - CATHERINE V. 5TH GRADE

September 21, 2006

Dear Mississippi Friend,

I'm sorry you lost your home and school in the hurricane Katrina. Don't lose your hope. You can still have dreams and goals. Make it possible to dream. Turn "impossible" to I'm possible! You need to believe in your self. I have hope in you. If your wondering were I'm from, I'm a third grader You can write me at my school.

your friend,
Jillian

The First Growing Field

A story of personal str...
A story about finding your...

My name is Chantelle.
But you could call me Shea.
I play softBall. I have
Brown eyes, Brown Hair, I am 11
years old about to turn 12 years
old in may, I am a girl.

Hurricane Katrina was a
disaster. I stayed for the
Hurricane. I was scared when
Hurricane Katrina Hit.

I want to ask you few
questins

What is your Favorite sport,
Daisy?
What is your eye Color?
What is your hair Color?
How old are you?

DEAR BEST FRIEND

I KNOW HOW YOU FEEL BUT I HOPE YOU
LIKE THIS BOOK.

I WANT TO BE FRIENDS WITH YOU FOREVER. I
HOPE YOU ARE OK.

MY NAME IS LAURA   I HOPE YOU
WRITE ME BACK.

Your Friend   Love Laura

I'M REALLY GLAD I GET A CHANCE TO WRITE YOU- YOU ARE IMPORTANT TO ME. - BRIANNA S. AGE 10

Dear Alessandra,

The ball and the baseball cards are showing that I like sports. The two dolphins things are showing how much I love dolphins!!!!! The pictures are showing me, the oldest, Lizzy, the middle child, and Maddison, the baby! These things are very special to me and I want you to have them. These things are reflecting how I am. Hope you like them.

Dear Anastasia,
Thank you so much for the long letter. I should probabably tell you a bit about myself. I have brown hair, hazel eyes, and I love to write, too! Your story was so inspiring to me, and I feel bad about complaining about things that now pale in comparison. We do have a shopping center here. Our town is small. It is divided into three parts, the village, Carmel-by-the-Sea, and the mouth of the valley (funny name, huh!). You worked so hard to help everyone around you when you were hurt, too. I would love to send you a few pictures of our town. Thank You for writing! It's great to talk to someone so similar to me.

Your New Friend,
Alessandra

87

Dear Mississippi friend,

Don't lose ANY hope your town will hit the come back trail.

I feel so spoiled here in CA. I'm sorry about your wondeful state. Please for the sake of us over here in CA, thing of the positive!!!! Whats your name? How old are you? I'm 10. Some peo Say Katrina is old news, I know better. How are you?

Your friend,
Alyssa K.

come back trail

mississippi

feb/2/07

Dear Alyssa,

My name is Bebecca. I am 9 years old. How old are you?

I got 19 feet of water in my house dring Hurricane Katrina. I lost everthing.

I'm in the 3nd grade. What grade are you in. My hobby is going swimming. What is your hobby. My favorite sport is softball. What is your favorite sport? My favorite colors are pink, gree,and brown. What are your favorite colors? My favorite food is chil cheese fries. What is you favorite food?

Pen Pal,
Becca

"Just know this... I'm here for you."

IF YOU ARE GOING THROUGH A HARD TIME WRITE TO ME AND I WILL COMFORT YOU. - MORGAN H

I hope you enjoyed this book but also learned that if you try, whatever you want to do or become in life will happen.

Never say something's impossible because that isn't true. Nothing's impossible unless you make it impossible. If you have a hard time doing the "impossible", try to remember NED. NED stands for;

N ever give up!!
E ncourage others!!
D o your best!!

Also you can turn "impossible" into im possible. Finally, remember that if you do your best and try your hardest nothing's impossible.

Kacie

Alana, Mississippi, Age 9
with her pen pal
Kylie, California, Age 9

"Will you be my friend?"

I liked that my pen pal was interested in hearing about such a life changing event. It shows that when someone we don't know shows concern when such devastation and destruction occurs... we can truly be one nation under God. — Kyle

Acknowledgements

It is only through the efforts and contributions of many talented individuals that this project was possible. I would like to recognize the following individuals, businesses and organizations who believed in this project and made their own invaluable contribution.

A very special thank you to the **Serimus Foundation** in Ft. Collins, Colorado for sponsoring the Letters From Katrina project. Through your generous grant the printing of this book, and the entire project, became a reality. Thank you for the "seeds you have sown" to make this project possible.

Friesens

A special thanks to the Friesens printing company for your contribution. Your team jumped at the opportunity to participate in this project for the families in Mississippi and made this a beautiful book. Thank you.

Our friends **Tommy, Judi and Brian Brooks** at BB's Barbeque and Snak Shak in Mississippi. Thank you for making sure we were always well fed while in Mississippi. We have never tasted better barbeque or felt more at home!

To **Cameron Way** at *Trent Studios* for donating your time and expertise to create the *Letters From Katrina* web site and for your generous donation to host the site. We could never have touched people across the globe with this project without your contribution.

A world of thanks to all of the great people at Hewlitt Packard and Lightning Source. Your involvement, commitment to leadership and corporate citizenship, is an inspiration and is going to change lives in Mississippi for generations.

Our friends at **Hollywood Casino** for providing our "home away from home" when traveling to Mississippi. Your hospitality is much appreciated.

This project would not have been possible without the number of schools, teachers, administrators, principals and children that shared their classroom time with us. With special thanks to **De Ross, Jeremy Rucker, Tonya Schwolert, Reenie Hollen, Tammy Raymond, Iris Sullivan, Jan White and Celeste Williams** for opening your door to us. The work each of you do every day changes the world!

Finally to photographer **Kim Lemaire** of *Ensemble Productions Photography*. You did so much more than take pictures for this project. Your unending belief, effort, energy and coordination made this project possible and brought completion to *Letters From Katrina*. Through your lens you captured the essence of the project and the compelling emotion of the children. The pictures you took are beautiful… but it was all you gave to the project that has made it a masterpiece. You have my unending gratitude. Thank you.

Letters From Katrina Marketing Team

Letters from Katrina owes special thanks to a talented **Colorado State University** marketing professor and a group of CSU marketing graduates who put their careers on hold and, instead, chose to donate their time, energy and marketing expertise to bring this project to the nation.

With a heart for children, and a passion for making a difference in the lives of families along the gulf coast, these individuals are responsible for developing and executing the marketing plan for *Letters from Katrina*.

Thank you to each of you for your invaluable contribution, your leadership, and for choosing to make a difference. Any business would be lucky to have you on their team!

Professor Joe Cannon

Kristin Armbrust	**Trevor McIntosh**	**Katie Moddelmog**	**Mike Newell**
Stewart Rettinger	**Ryan Rusler**	**Richard Shinazy**	**Holly McSwain**

To **Greg Snider** at Blu Sky Media Group for donating your distribution services and allowing this book to reach the book trade for the families of Mississippi. To **Gwyn Snider** for volunteering your time and talent to design this book. Your creative talents delivered the perfect touch to this project.

To cover designer, and my right hand man, **Rob Aukerman**. I have never met someone as talented or as selfless. Your ability to hear an idea and turn it into perfection is pure magic. There are not enough words to express my gratitude to you.

For **Peri Basseri** - Thank you for using your creative talent in producing our *Letters from Katrina* slide show, and for donating the DVD's that helped make it possible to get the word out about the project. You offered to help from day one before completely understanding the project. You are a true friend and have been a wonderful asset.

Mark and Bernadette Smith - Thank you so much for helping with web site issues and for making it possible to send huge files coast to coast. You helped on so many levels, thank you for being my friends.

Elizabeth Sills and **Elena Patrice** of *EE Publishing* - the "laugh friendly" company for sharing your vision to produce *Letters from Katrina*. One measure of our lives is the quality of people we encounter along the way. I am thankful our paths crossed.

FedEx

Thanks to the **FedEx** team in Ft. Collins, Colorado for donating your services and allowing us to ship books, letters and supplies back and forth.

DO YOU REMEMBER THE MAGIC OF YOUR FIRST BOOK?

To **Mary Beth**, and the rest of the First Book team, for working with us to find the incredible people of Mississippi. Your work across the country is an inspiration for all of us.

Each of you in the **Ft. Collins Breakfast Rotary Club** are amazing and truly exemplify the Rotary motto… "service above self." Thank you for the donation that launched this project. I will be back soon to get rid of my red badge!